TH WRITER'S GUIDE TO CRITIQUE GROUPS

Linda Griffin

ImaJinn Books
A Division of ImaJinn
Hickory Corners, Michigan
877-625-3592

First Printing 1999

Cover design by Patricia Lazarus

ISBN: 1-893896-00-5
Library of Congress Catalog Number: 99-71628

A special thank you to Lisa Turner, Orysia Earhart, Pat Lazarus and Laurie Kuna. Thanks for helping make the dream come true!

4/29/01
John —
It was great
meeting you.
Happy
creating!

Laura Guffin

P.S. Don't forget to send me your "dream" book!

Table of Contents

INTRODUCTION

When I first started writing, I had never met a writer, and I didn't know anything about writers' organizations. All I had was a dream to publish a novel. I bought a "how-to" book on writing, and I used it as a bible. When I finished my first manuscript, I knew I was in trouble. The shortest novel I'd seen was approximately 200 pages. My double-spaced manuscript was 126 pages. I hadn't written a book. I'd written a short story, and not a very good one.

Realizing I drastically needed help, I headed for the book stores and the library. I brought home every "how-to-write" book I could find. I studied the basics of writing, and, over the next three months, I read approximately 300 novels in the genre in which I wanted to publish. My studying and reading helped. My second manuscript was better, or maybe I should say "longer," but I knew it still wasn't good enough to be published. Undaunted, I started a third novel. I wanted to be a writer, and I knew it would happen. I just had to work harder and believe in myself.

Fortunately for me, I also joined a national writers organization. Through that organization, I met another writer living in the same town. She literally changed my writing life by teaching me the value of a good critique. Through her critiques, she made me aware of problems in my story, as well as the positive aspects of my writing. Her praise gave me the self-confidence I needed to sustain my dream of becoming a published writer, and her critiques made me a better writer.

Then my husband got a new job across the country, which meant I had to leave my one and only writing friend. I was devastated. How could I possibly find another writer who could give me such wonderful critiques? It wasn't as hard as I expected because I knew what I wanted and needed from a critique. By understanding my needs, I was able to find other writers who could fulfill them.

Over the years, I've met talented writers whose writing could benefit from joining a critique group, but they were afraid to do so because they feared putting their writing on the line. As one writer said to me, "I have an aversion to spilling mine or someone else's blood over written words." I've also met writers who have joined critique groups only to be disappointed and frustrated because the group wasn't what they expected or needed. Either the members of the group were "too critical" or they weren't "critical enough." In all three instances, the writers share the same problem. They don't know how to look for the proper critique group, because they had not determined what they needed from a critique group.

That's why I've written *The Writer's Guide to Critique Groups*. This is *not* a "how-to" book. It's a guide to help writers determine if they will benefit from a critique group and, if so, what type of group they should join. It also offers critique alternatives for the writer who isn't ready for, or doesn't have time for, a group.

Hopefully, by the time you finish reading *The Writer's Guide to Critique Groups* you'll know how to get—and give—a good critique without shedding yours or someone else's blood in the process.

CRITIQUE BASICS

Regardless of whether you write fiction or nonfiction, writing is a profession that requires you to relearn your job every day. You know the basics of writing—like grammar, structure, plot and characterization—but every time you sit down to write you face a blank computer screen or a blank piece of paper. You must fill this blank space with scenes you've never written before and will never write again. More importantly, each of those scenes must be so unique and exciting that it will thrill agents, editors, and ultimately readers.

When working at "regular" jobs, you work with people who either affirm you're doing a good job or help you if you're having difficulties. In writing, however, there's no one to give you affirmation or, if your writing isn't the masterpiece you want it to be, offer you advice on how to fix it. Some writers have enough self-confidence to handle this isolation. Other writers both want and need input on their work. This is why many writers consider joining a writing critique group that meets on a regular basis.

Before you enter into the critique arena, however,

you need to determine what a critique means, and if you're emotionally and physically equipped to handle the consequences it entails. One of those consequences is that, if you ask other writers to critique your work, they will expect you to critique their work. If you join a critique group, you will not only have several people critiquing your work, but you'll be critiquing the work of several people. This can be time-consuming. It can also be ego-bruising if you aren't ready to accept criticism on your writing, since one of the definitions of the word critique is "to criticize." Finally, you need to determine if you are able to provide constructive criticism to others on their work.

The   most important criteria to apply to any aspect of your writing, including a critique of your work, is that the activity *must* enhance your writing in some way. Don't let yourself be forced into a critique group because other writers say you should belong to one. Join because, after reviewing the pros and cons of critique groups addressed in this book, you've determined this is an activity that will make you a better writer.

With that said, let's get down to critique basics.

THE BASICS

You've poured your heart and soul into writing a story. Now you're done and you're not sure if the story is as good (or as bad) as you think. Or maybe you've written two or three chapters of your story, and now you're stuck because you don't know where to go. Another problem you may face is that you have a story inside you begging to be written, but you can't seem to find enough self-discipline to write on a regular basis.

All of these scenarios are excellent reasons to join a critique group. You may be hesitant, however, to take that step. What if the other members of the group hate your writing style? Or what if they love your work and you hate theirs?

If you think getting and giving a critique is an emotional landmine ready to explode in your face, you're right. No one likes criticism, and a critique not only requires you to accept criticism but to do so with grace. So why would you subject yourself to such a demoralizing act?

You need to answer that question with another question, which is: *Would I rather get criticism from other writers, or a rejection letter from an editor or an agent?* Belonging to a critique group does not guarantee that you won't be rejected by editors and agents, but membership in a good critique group should increase your chances of getting published.

Another reason for belonging to a critique group is that you can gain a perspective on your work that you're unable to obtain on your own. Indeed, one of the most common questions asked by writers is: *Why can I see the problems in someone else's work, but I can't see them in my own?* The answer is as simple as the cliche: *You can't see the forest for the trees.* You're so busy laying the foundation of your story with all those thousands of little words that create the "big picture" that you can lose sight of the big picture altogether.

Despite the positive aspects of a critique group, there are also negative ones. You will give up a significant amount of your writing time. You are also setting yourself up for ego-bashing, and placing yourself in a position to ego-bash someone else. Some writers aren't emotionally equipped for either "bashing" process.

To determine whether or not you're equipped to give and receive critiques, you need to ask yourself why you want a critique and what you hope to gain from one. You also need to ask yourself if you are capable of reciprocating by providing another writer with a constructive critique. This chapter should help you answer those questions.

ASKING FOR A CRITIQUE

You've decided you want to join a critique group. Before you take this step, ask yourself these questions and answer them honestly. Remember, this isn't a test you can pass or fail.

QUESTIONS

- **Why do I want a critique?**

  A.   I want constructive criticism that will help me develop a publishable manuscript.

  B.   I want affirmation that my writing is good.

- **What do I expect from a critique?**

  A.   I expect to receive an analysis of characterization, plot and structure.

  B.   I expect to receive line editing, to include spell checking, grammar correction, etc.

  C.   I expect to receive both.

- **How should I respond when I get the critique back?**

  A.   Read or listen to the comments and analyze them. Then, after I've had some time to consider them, incorporate those that I feel are appropriate into my book.

  B.   Discuss the reasons why my characters have done what they've done with the critiquer, so that she/he will understand my reasoning.

- **I've received several critiques, and I've looked over all the comments. Now, what do I do?**

> A.   Incorporate all suggestions into my story.
> B.   Analyze the suggestions, determining which are appropriate to my story and which are not. Then do my revisions.

- **I've done my revisions. Now what should I do?**

> A.   Ask the person(s) who critiqued my manuscript to read it again.
> B.   Ask another person to read it.
> C.   Mail it off to an editor or an agent.

ANSWERS

- **Why do I want a critique?**

> A.   I want constructive criticism that will help me develop a publishable manuscript.
> B.   I want affirmation that my writing is good.

If B is your answer, give your book to your mother or your best friend, who will love anything you write, even if it's bad. All writers need affirmation that their writing is good, particularly when they first start writing. There is nothing wrong with this. Indeed, it's healthy, because praise will encourage you to continue working toward your dream.

A good critique, however, is not designed to stroke your ego. It should provide affirmation of your writing skills, but its purpose is to find problems in your story and help you figure out solutions to those problems. If all you really want is some ego stroking, don't ask other writers to take time away from their own writing to read your manuscript. You will resent their criticisms, and they will resent giving up their time when you didn't want their honest opinion. If praise is all you need at this point in your writing career, stay away from critique groups.

- **What do you expect from a critique?**

    A. I expect to receive an analysis of characterization, plot and structure.
    B. I expect to receive line editing, to include spell checking, grammar correction, etc.
    C. I expect to receive both.

If your answer is B or C, make sure you communicate this to the critique group before you give them your manuscript. Additionally, make sure the group does line editing before joining them. Many writers do not do line editing because they don't have the time or because they aren't particularly good at it themselves. They might make minor corrections to a manuscript, such as penciling in a word that was left out or circling a word that has been used repetitively, but they really don't care how you use your commas. They want to focus on the evenness of your plot line, the overall structure of the story, and the characters: their goals, motivations, and internal and external conflicts. If you have not specifically asked for line editing, do not expect to receive it.

- **How should I respond when I get the critique back?**

> A.   Read or listen to the comments and analyze them. Then, after I've had some time to consider them, incorporate those that I feel are appropriate into my book.
>
> B.   Discuss the reasons why my characters have done what they've done with the critiquer(s), so that she/he will understand my reasoning.

If you answered B, then you probably didn't want a critique in the first place. You wanted affirmation, and your feelings are hurt because you didn't get it. When someone does a critique, they are giving you their *opinion*, and arguing with them about their opinion is non-productive. Even if you can convince them that your motives were valid, your method obviously didn't work because they didn't "get it" during the initial reading. Of it they did "get it," they obviously didn't like it. The simple truth is they don't care why you did what you did. They're simply telling you that in their *opinion* it did not work. If you feel they're wrong, discard their opinion and move on.

- **I've received several critiques, and I've looked over all the comments. Now, what do I do?**

    A.   Incorporate all suggestions into my story.
    B.   Analyze the suggestions, determining which are appropriate to my story and which are not. Then do my revisions.

Your answer should be B. As already stated, when you ask for a critique you are asking for an *opinion*. Ideally, the person(s) reading your work will be objective, but the reality is that all opinions are subjective. This is why you may love a certain book, and someone else hates it. Only you know your characters and your storyline in depth, and only you can determine if a suggestion is appropriate. If you try to incorporate everyone's suggestions into a book, you'll lose the integrity of the book because you cannot please everyone. A good rule to follow is, if two people note the same problem, then you should take a hard look at it because it probably does need to be fixed.

- **I've done my revisions. Now what should I do?**

A.   Ask the person(s) who critiqued my manuscript to read it again.

B.   Ask another person to read it.

C.   Mail it off to an editor or an agent.

Your answer should be B or C, depending upon how confident you feel about the book. Be wary, however, of asking another person to read it because they will come back with new suggestions. So, only resort to B if you feel the book is still not ready to be sent to a publisher, and you can't figure out why.

The reason you shouldn't choose the first option is because, once someone's read your book, they've already formed their opinion of it. They're too close to the story to provide you with any more valuable input, and this is a common problem I've seen in critique groups. They've read the original version of your manuscript and your 200 revisions. Then you give your manuscript to someone outside the critique group, and they find problems you feel your group should have caught. The reason the group didn't catch those problems is because they're read the story so many times they can no longer see it objectively.

The solution to this problem is simple. When a critique group forms, each member should choose one person in the group to read her revisions. Even then, that person shouldn't be required to read more than two revisions of a scene. When you rewrite a scene over and over again, you edit out all the magic that was there in the first place. To stop that from happening, if you can't revise a scene to your satisfaction after two rewrites, move on to the next scene. You can come back to the problematic scene after you've had enough time away from it to gain some perspective.

Another reason to have one person in the group critique your revisions is that, when you've finally completed your manuscript and you're ready to market it, the rest of the group can read the entire story with an open mind. This means they'll give you excellent critiques because the story will still be fresh enough for them to enjoy reading it.

DO YOU KNOW HOW TO CRITIQUE?

As stated earlier, when you ask someone to critique your work, you can expect them to ask you to critique their work in return. Giving a critique can be as intimidating as asking for one. What if you hate their work? What if you offend them and they retaliate by unfairly tearing your manuscript apart?

The best way to answer these "what if" scenarios is to determine if you know how to give a critique. You don't need to be a critique expert to evaluate someone's work, but you do need to decide if you can offer an objective and constructive critique. In order to determine the answer to that question, ask yourself the following questions and, again, answer them honestly.

QUESTIONS

- Can I read a manuscript objectively, or will I be tempted to rewrite it with my own voice and style?

- Do I know the difference between a critique and line editing?

- What is my writing forte, and what are my weaknesses? Am I willing to explain my writing weaknesses to another writer, or will I lie to "save face"?

- Am I familiar enough with and like the genre enough to give a fair opinion on the manuscript?

- Do I expect any or all of my suggestions to be followed? If they aren't, will I be angry?

- Can I give constructive criticism? Am I comfortable about sitting down with the writer and reviewing my comments face-to-face and in detail?

- Is my plotting skill good enough that I can offer viable suggestions to fix problems I see in the manuscript?

- Does critiquing another writer's work make me feel powerful or superior?

ANSWERS

- Can I read a manuscript objectively, or will I be tempted to rewrite it with my own voice and style?

When you critique someone's work, your job is to objectively look at the manuscript and decide if the characters are properly motivated and sympathetic. Is the plot strong and even? If it's a novel, is the structure smooth? Does every scene propel the story forward? Is there too much narrative or dialogue? Is there enough description to make you feel as if you're in the setting?

If you find yourself unable to address these issues without rewriting or re-plotting the book the way you would write it, then you should not critique until you learn how to maintain your objectivity. One of the ways to learn how to give a good critique is to give yourself a good self-critique. See the chapter on *Blueprint for a Critique* for more details.

Now, let's review the questions.

- **Do I know the difference between a critique and line editing?**

A critique involves characters, plot and structure. Unless a writer specifically asks for line editing, you should not concern yourself with their grammar, sentence structure, and word usage. If you feel someone has a problem with basic grammar, you should point it out, but do so gently. Your job is to encourage, not discourage. Also, is this a first draft? If so, you can assume the writer will cleanup the manuscript during revision. Your job is to look at the meat of the story, find problems and offer solutions.

- **What is my writing forte, and what are my weaknesses? Am I willing to explain my writing weaknesses to another writer, or will I lie to "save face"?**

All writers have strengths and weaknesses in their writing. Before you critique someone's work, you should find out if they have a specific area they want addressed. For instance, if a writer is concerned that the plot is not strong enough or it's too complicated, and your biggest weakness is plotting; you are not the one to offer advice. You should explain to the writer that you also have this problem and sympathize with her frustration. Then tell her you probably wouldn't be much help with the problem and she should turn to someone else for assistance. Also, tell her what your writing strengths are and offer her assistance in those areas if she needs it.

• **Am I familiar enough with, and do I like the genre enough, to give a fair opinion on the manuscript?**

If you are not familiar with a genre, or you do not particularly care for a specific genre, then you should not critique those types of manuscripts. It isn't fair to you or the writer. You may end up being unjustly critical, or you may offer advice that is incorrect for that genre. Explain to the writer that you do not read mysteries or action adventure or romance and, therefore, you don't feel qualified to give them a good critique.

• **Do I expect any or all of my suggestions to be followed? If they aren't, will I be angry?**

This may seem like a ridiculous question, but it is a question you need to carefully consider. When you critique someone's work, you are giving them part of your valuable time. Human nature says you will want affirmation that sharing your time was worth it, and the best way to receive that affirmation is to have the writer follow your advice.

Whenever you give a critique, remind yourself that you are giving the writer your opinion on his work. This is not your story, and he is not obligated to follow your suggestions. For you to be offended or angry if he discards your input is unjustified, albeit understandable. After all, you worked so hard for nothing! But the only time your anger is justified is if you've taken time away from your own writing to critique a story and then you learn the writer only wanted you to tell him how wonderful his writing is. If you do find yourself in this situation, chalk it up to experience and forget about it. It's a waste of energy to be angry, and you'll be better off putting that energy into your own writing. If, however, that person asks you for another critique, politely tell him that you don't have the time.

- **Can I give constructive criticism? Am I comfortable about sitting down with the writer and reviewing my comments face-to-face and in detail?**

As stated earlier in the book, the foundation of a

critique is criticism. However, there is constructive criticism and there is destructive criticism. If you agree to critique someone's work, this does not give you the right to attack her writing or question her talent. Whenever you give a critique, you should always offer a possible solution to areas you feel have problems. If you can't come up with solutions on your own, seek the advice of someone whom you feel may be able to offer some solutions.

There is a "Golden Rule" for a good critique, and that's that you should always find something in a manuscript to praise, no matter how awful you think the story is. This is particularly true if you're working with a novice writer. Don't assume that if, in your opinion, a manuscript "stinks" that the writer doesn't have talent. It takes awhile for the novice writer to understand a novel's form and structure. The person you attack today could be a best seller five years from now, and you might need help from her.

If at all possible, give your comments on a manuscript face-to-face, even if they are hard criticisms. It's easier to be unkind when writing something on paper. It's also easier to misinterpret what someone says on paper, because you don't see their facial expressions and hear the tone of their voice.

If you must deliver your comments in writing, put them aside for a day or two before sending them. Then sit down and read them, asking yourself how you would feel if you received this letter. If you are using a lot of exclamation points or buzz words that might incite anger, rewrite your comments. Avoid using the word "I" in your comments, such as "I would have," "If I were writing this story," etc. Also, avoid phrases such as "you need to do this" or "You should have done that." Try to couch criticism with questions, such as, "Have you considered. . .? Would it be possible. . . ? What would happen if. . .?"

- **Is my plotting skill good enough that I can offer viable suggestions to fix plot problems I see in the manuscript?**

Plotting is a difficult endeavor. Most writers can read a manuscript and spot plot problems, but some writers only sense that "something is wrong" with the story. Their plotting skill isn't developed enough to define what that "something" is, let alone how to fix it. If you can't define a plot problem or you can't see a viable solution to it, you need to work on your plotting skills because, if you can't define a problem in someone else's work, you probably can't see the problems in your own work. Also, the most frequent critique criticism is a plot problem. You should be able to define these problems and provide the writer with two, and preferably three, ideas on how she might fix it.

- **Does critiquing another writer's work make me feel powerful or superior?**

If you answer "yes" to this question—and remember, you are supposed to answer honestly—do not join a critique group. Answering yes doesn't mean you're a bad person. It simply means that you are unable to maintain the objectivity you'll need to critique effectively. You're probably more suited to a one-on-one critique, and you should consider getting a critique partner, as outlined in the chapter entitled *Critique Partners*.

HOW TO CHOOSE (OR FORM) A CRITIQUE GROUP

You've just gone through the questions in the previous chapter, and you've decided that you're ready for a critique group. So how do you go about finding the right critique group to join?

If you want a positive experience that will enhance your writing, choosing the right critique group is one of the most important decisions you'll make in your writing career. A good critique group not only provides you with insight into your work, but it also gives you emotional support. Writing is an emotional roller coast ride. If an editor or agent asks to see your manuscript, you're riding high and your critique group celebrates with you. If an editor or agent has turned down your manuscript, you're about as low as you can get, and your critique group is there to commiserate and boost your spirits so you can put the rejection behind you and move on with your writing.

If you want to join an already organized group, ask if you can attend two or three critique sessions before you make up your mind about joining. While you're at the sessions, ask yourself the following:

QUESTIONS

- Are members required to produce a certain amount of work in order to belong to the group?

- How many members are in the group? Will I have enough time to review all of their work based upon the minimum page requirement?

- What type of writers are in the group?

- Does the group also brainstorm if members are having problems with their current project or are starting a new project?

- Do I like the dynamics of the group?

- I can't find a critique group I feel meets my needs. What should I do?

ANSWERS

• Are members required to produce a certain amount of work in order to belong to the group?

This is one of the most critical questions you need to answer before joining any critique group. The most successful critique groups are those whose unpublished members get published. In most instances, these groups require their members to bring at least five new manuscript pages to each meeting. This may sound like an unreasonable requirement, but there are two excellent reasons for this rule.

The first reason is that writing is hard work and, unless there's a deadline of some sort, it's easy to find good reasons not to write. You may need to clean house or pay the bills or prepare a budget for the year or clean out the closets or go to lunch with a friend or . . .

You can see that there are hundreds of valid reasons for not writing, and this is probably the number one reason why many talented writers never get published. They simply don't have the self-discipline, or the willingness to sacrifice something else, in order to write on a regular basis. If, however, a writer is required to produce a certain amount of work in order to belong to a critique group, she will generally meet that requirement.

The second reason is a morale factor.   As

discussed before, a critique is a critical review of your work. If everyone in a group is getting criticized, then everyone in the group is on equal footing. If, however, a member of a group is constantly critical of everyone's work but never produces any work of her own to be criticized, the members of the group will begin to resent that person. It doesn't mean the person's opinion isn't valid. It's simply human nature for people to feel that if someone is going to criticize them, they should have the right to criticize back.

If you don't feel you're ready to commit to a minimum number of pages for every meeting, then you may want to consider joining a social group rather than a critique group. There's nothing wrong with joining a social group. The main reason for going to any meeting is to enhance your writing. If a social group provides you with the stimulus you need to write, then they've fulfilled their purpose.

- **How many members are in the group? Will I have enough time to review all of their work based upon the minimum page requirement?**

Belonging to a critique group can be time consuming. Let's say you belong to a group with five members. The group meets once a week, and all of you write at least five pages a week. You would have to critique twenty pages a week, as well as write your own five pages. If you have a member that generates fifty pages a week, you'd have to critique those pages plus whatever pages the others generate. If you have two prolific writers in the group, you could be critiquing 100 or more pages a week.

When you are analyzing your ability to participate effectively in a critique group, you need to determine how many pages a week you can review and still accomplish your own goals. If you're like most writers, you hold down a full-time job and have a family to care for, so your writing time is limited. If belonging to a critique group will take too much time away from your own writing, you may want to consider having a critique partner rather than joining a critique group. Critique partners are discussed in the next chapter.

• What type of writers are in the group?

An ideal critique group will be composed of writers who are writing for the same genre. There are significant differences in the way genres are written. For instance, if a writer is writing a traditional mystery, the mystery will be the focus of the story, but if a writer is writing a romantic mystery, the romance will be the focus of the story. If a mystery writer is not familiar with the romantic mystery genre, he may give bad advice by trying to bring the mystery to the forefront. If a romantic mystery writer isn't familiar with traditional mysteries, he may give the mystery writer bad advice by trying to make him insert a romantic element or bring an existing romantic element to the forefront. A mixture of writers from different genres can work together effectively, but they need a basic understanding of each others' genres.

- **Does the group also brainstorm if members are having problems with their current project or are starting a new project?**

Most critique groups do more than just evaluate each others' written work. They'll also brainstorm plot ideas on current and new projects. Brainstorming, however, will increase the length of a meeting. If you're strapped for time, you may want to look for a critique partner.

- **Do you like the dynamics of the group?**

This is the most critical question you need to ask yourself, because it will determine if you feel comfortable in a group. If you are shy and/or prefer to receive and give tactful remarks, you won't feel comfortable in a group whose members say, "This scene sucks swamp water!" On the other hand, if you're a person who prefers to receive—and give—the "swamp water" analogy, you'll feel inhibited within a tactful group.

- I can't find a critique group I feel meets my needs. What should I do?

If you can't find an already organized critique group, then you should consider starting your own. Use the above questions to select group members and establish guidelines.

A word of advice: The biggest mistake new groups make is letting the membership get too large. Remember, when the group meets, you will discuss each member's work. In most instances, it will take at least twenty to thirty minutes for everyone in the group to give input on one person's work and for that person to ask questions. A good rule to follow is to start out with three to five members. After you've worked together for a while, you can determine if the group can be larger without creating a hardship on the membership.

Remember. It's easy to make a group larger. It's nearly impossible to make a group smaller.

CRITIQUE PARTNERS

If you've gone through the above chapters and feel that you either don't have the time for a group or you're a person who can't handle the critical aspect of a group, you may want to consider a critique partner. A writer once told me that you should take more time selecting a critique partner than you should a spouse. I'm not sure I'd go quite that far, but it is critical that you select a good partner. Remember, this person will be replacing the group, and you should receive as much help from a partner as you would from a group. To select a good partner, follow the criteria listed below.

CRITIQUE PARTNER CRITERIA

- **A critique partner should be a person you know and whose judgement you trust.**

If you don't know someone who falls into this category, look for other writers who are also looking for someone to look at their work. Exchange work with these writers two or three times. If you find a writer whom you feel gives you the type of critique you need, and she seems to respond positively to your critiques, approach her about forming a critique partnership.

- **Just like in a critique group, it's ideal to have a critique partner who writes in the same genre you do.**

This isn't absolutely necessary. It is, however, essential that this person know and understand your genre. As stated above, you need to trust this person's judgement, and that's the main criteria you should use when selecting a critique partner.

- **Establish a minimum number of pages to exchange each week.**

As with a critique group, a critique partnership should put you under a deadline that will force you to write.

ADVANTAGES OF A CRITIQUE PARTNER

The advantages of having a critique partner over belonging to a critique group are as follows:

- **Time.**

    Even if your critique partner writes fifty pages a week, you will probably spend less time critiquing her work than you would with a critique group. When you're dealing with one manuscript, you don't have to change plots and tone, so your concentration is focused on one story. Also, you will spend less time going over each other's comments. Remember, in a critique group, it will take at least twenty to thirty minutes *per person* to go over everyone's comments and allow the writer to ask questions. When you're working one-on-one, you can probably exchange your comments in thirty minutes or less.

- **Schedule flexibility.**

    If you deal with one person, it's easier to change a meeting date or, if it's inconvenient for you to meet, you can do your critiques over the telephone. You can even agree to exchange your writing on a daily basis, which will allow you to review each other's writing in small chunks rather than in one large chunk. If both you and your critique partner have access to e-mail, you could live across the country from each other and still be able to review each other's work on a daily basis. As you can see, schedule flexibility is unlimited with a critique partner.

- **Limited input.**
  When you deal with a group, you receive several opinions on your work. You'll have to sift through the comments and choose which ones you feel are pertinent to your story. With a critique partner, you have one opinion to consider.

DISADVANTAGES OF A CRITIQUE PARTNER

The disadvantages of a critique partner over a group are:

- **Limited input.**
  You only have one opinion on your work. When you're having problems with your story, multiple opinions will provide you with several ideas to pursue. This broadens the scope of possibilities in your work.

- **Hurt Feelings.**

  It's easier to take offense when dealing with one person instead of a group. When you deal with a group and one person finds fault with an aspect of your writing, others of the group will often disagree. Also, in a group atmosphere, the person giving you the criticism or to whom you're giving criticism doesn't feel as if she's being attacked, which can be a problem with a one-on-one critique partner.

- **Easier Excuses.**

  It's easier to make excuses to one person for not writing than it is to a group.

- **Abandonment.**

  If something happens in your critique partner's life that makes it impossible for him or her to critique your work for several weeks, you can feel abandoned and frustrated. With a group, if one person is unable to function for a period of time, the rest of the group will still be there to review your work.

  When choosing a critique partner, you should ask yourself the same questions you would ask about joining a critique group. If you and your critique partner are close friends, you also need to consider if criticizing each other's work will have an impact on your friendship. A good critique partner will ruthlessly tell you what's wrong with your work. If you're going through a bad writing spell where nothing you put down on paper is working, the constant criticism from a friend will sting.

Some writers belong to a critique group and also have a critique partner separate from the group. They often use the partner to review their daily work, which they then revise before presenting it to the group at their weekly meeting. Some writers do the exact opposite, using the group to provide input and then giving the revised version to the partner.

If you have the time for both methods of critique, go for it. It can't be emphasized enough that the reason to get involved in the critique process is to make yourself a better and/or a more productive writer.

BLUEPRINT FOR
A CRITIQUE

Have you decided you aren't ready for a critique group or partner? Or have you decided you want to join a group or find a partner, but you aren't sure if your critique skills are good enough to evaluate someone else's work?

If your answer to either of those questions is "yes," this chapter will provide you with a blueprint to a good critique. Using the techniques listed below, you can perform a self-critique on your own work which will help you develop the necessary skills to evaluate someone else's work. You can also use this blueprint when evaluating another writer's work, which will help you ensure that you're finding all the problems.

THE CRITIQUE PROCESS

For the purposes of this chapter, we're going to assume that you do not belong to a critique group or have a critique partner, and you want to perform a self-critique. We're also going to assume the manuscript is in the final draft, although you may use any of these steps for evaluating scenes as you write them.

With that in mind, let's say you've finished your book. So what's the next step in a self-critique?

- **Put the manuscript away for at least one and preferably two or more weeks.**

Your first instinct when finishing your book is to immediately mail it to an editor and/or agent. After all, it takes editors and/or agents *forever* to respond. The faster you mail it to them, the faster you'll hear from them.

You're right. You will hear faster, but you'll probably receive a rejection letter. In order to do a good line editing and self-critique of your manuscript, you need to distance yourself from it. Remember, you've been so busy writing those thousands of little words to build the big picture that you've lost sight of the forest for the trees.

If you can't trust yourself to leave the manuscript alone, get it out of the house, even if it means copying it to a disk and deleting it off your computer. Then ask your spouse, significant other, or friend to take your disk or your manuscript in to work with him. If your manuscript is on a computer and you really can't bear the thought of it leaving the house, have someone you trust transfer the manuscript to another file and assign a secret password to it. You could even mail your manuscript, disk, or secret password to a friend across the country and ask her to mail it right back to you. By the time you get the material back, your week will be over. Whatever you decide to do, give an extra copy of your manuscript to a friend or family member in case the one you mailed or secured gets lost or damaged.

So what are you going to do during that week or two while you're distancing yourself from your manuscript? You're going to read. Choose a genre completely different from what you've written, so you won't be tempted to compare the writer's work with yours. Also, by reading another genre, you'll see story structure in a new light, and this should help you see structural problems in your manuscript.

IDENTIFY CHARACTER GOALS, MOTIVATIONS AND CONFLICTS

- **Your week is finally over, and you're ready to start your self-critique. The first thing you need to do is identify the goals, motivations,**

and internal and external conflicts of your characters.

Most writers feel that the structural backbone of any good story is characterization. At some point in the initial writing phase of your manuscript, you should have developed a list that delineates the goals, motivations, and internal and external conflicts for each of your characters.

Pull this list out and re-familiarize yourself with it, or if you haven't made a list, now's a good time to do so. As you read through your manuscript, you'll want to make sure the threads of your characters' goals, motivations, and internal and external conflicts run through the manuscript. For instance, you have a character named John. John's terrified of fire, but somewhere in the book he'll have to rush into a burning building to save his child. Don't wait until the fire to announce that John's afraid of fire. Build it into the story, so that when John has to run into that building, the readers are sitting on the edges of their seats wondering if he'll be able to overcome his fear to save the child.

If your characters' goals, motivations and conflicts are going to change in the story, make sure that the reasons for change are clearly defined. For instance, John's original goal was to get custody of his child, and that goal is motivated by revenge—*How dare his ex-wife leave him! He'll show her. He'll take custody of their daughter, and she'll never see the child again!* By the end of the book, he may come to realize that his child belongs with its mother, and that he's been blaming his ex-wife for problems that were actually his fault. You don't want this realization to suddenly hit him at the end of the book. You want to show the events—and his reaction to them—that will ultimately lead him to these revelations.

If you aren't sure how to develop goals, motivations, and internal and external conflicts, an excellent book on the subject is *GMC: Goal, Motivation & Conflict: The Building Blocks of Good Fiction,* written by Debra Dixon and published by Gryphon Books for Writers. Information on ordering Ms. Dixon's book may be found in the back of this book.

ESTABLISH CHARACTER CHART

Establish a character chart of the book. You can do this on a wide sheet of paper, on the computer, or on a poster board. Create a column for each chapter. Now, make a column on the left that lists all the characters in your book.

Once you have your characters listed, go down the list, placing a check mark beneath each chapter where he/she appears. This will tell you where each character appears, and who interacts with them. This should help you figure out if you need to beef up a character or downsize a minor character. Or, perhaps a minor character is in reality a major character, and you need to make changes to reflect that change.

After you've completed your chapter list, take a red pencil, a magic marker, or a heavy graphics line (if you're using the computer) and divide the chapters into the beginning, the middle and the end. This will show you where each of your characters first appears and who is finishing the book. It should also help you see a balance, or imbalance, of the characters in the story.

Here is a computerized example of this process.

| CHARACTER | BEGINNING | | | MIDDLE | | | END | | |
	ONE	TWO	THREE	FOUR	FIVE	SIX	SEVEN	EIGHT	NINE
Susan (Protagonist)	x	x	x	x	x	x	x	x	x
John (Antogonist)	x		x	x		x	x	x	x
Tom	x		x		x		x		x
Jane		x	x		x	x	x		x
Harry			x	x		x			

EVALUATE BEGINNING

Once you've established your character chart and know who starts where and when, you can start evaluating the beginning of the story. Ask yourself the following questions:

- Where does the story begin? Is it in the middle of action? Is what the protagonist believes to be true about himself being challenged or threatened? Make sure your protagonist has something happen to her in the first chapter that starts the clock ticking.

- What is the dramatic event in the beginning of the book that will threaten the main character and cause a change in his or her self-image?

- What is your main character's terrible secret that, if revealed, will cause him or someone he loves irreparable harm?

- What is his goal? This is the problem to be solved at the end of the book. How does your character intend to solve the problem in the beginning of the book? By the end of the book, he won't solve it the way he originally intended because he will grow and change as he faces the obstacles in his way to the goal. He will, however, need a plan of action at the start of the book.

- Are you happy with your opening scene? If not, you may be starting the book before the action begins. Look for the first action scene that hooks your interest. Should this be the opening scene? Can the information you're providing before the action scene be given in small flashbacks throughout the book? The most common problem with beginnings is the writer's attempt to explain to the reader the background leading up to the story. The reader doesn't care about background. She wants to leap into action from page one.

- Did you set your clock so it will tick to an inevitable end? Every story needs some form of a ticking clock, although it doesn't have to involve time. Your ticking clock can be that John can't get custody of his child until he can prove his ex-wife an unfit mother.

EVALUATE MIDDLE

The middle of your story is where the reader sees the conflict increase. Every time your protagonist turns around, he's faced with another obstacle that appears insurmountable. He's also going through changes because his obstacles are teaching him lessons that will change the way he views his world. Keeping these thoughts in mind, ask yourself the following questions when critiquing the middle of your story.

- Is the conflict increasing? Conflict is critical to your story. Your protagonist must constantly be facing obstacles that appear insurmountable. Perhaps John convinces a judge to give him temporary custody of his child, only to have the child run away. Now his wife has ammunition to prove him an unfit father. He tries to prove she's wrong, but, every time he turns around, something else comes up to suggest he is unfit.

- Are the characters changing? Why? Are the changes visible? Your characters must undergo some form of change in the story. These changes should be subtle but visible. We discussed previously that John might discover at the end of the story that his child belongs with its mother, and he (John) caused many of the problems that ended his marriage. These are positive changes. Another example might be Sarah Conner in the movie *The Terminator*. Sarah starts out as an innocent young woman with an average life. By the end of the movie, she's become a hardened warrior who will fight to the death to save her son and, hopefully, change the world so the future won't be as grim as she's told it is. Again, it's a positive change, but with a dark overtone.

- Are the character's old motivations and goals replaced by new ones? Your character will start out with goals and motivations, but they'll be replaced with new ones as the story progresses. Remember, John's original goal was to get custody of his child. Then his child ran away from him. Now his new goal will be to find his child before something bad happens.

- Are the characters overreacting? When you look at your scenes, make sure they are dramatic and not melodramatic. Suppose John just found out his child has run away. We know he got custody of the child out of revenge. His first reaction would probably be to think his ex-wife has taken the child. When he realizes, however, that his ex-wife isn't involved, he's going to be stunned, possibly angry, and hopefully worried and guilt-ridden. After all, because of his petty behavior his child has run away, and something terrible could happen. John, however, isn't going to tear at his hair and his clothes and burst into tears, while wailing that this is all his fault. In the first place, this is not typical male behavior. When it comes to emotions, most men are self-contained. Even though John may blame himself, he will not waste time flagellating himself. He'll come up with a course of action to find his child. At the same time, his ex-wife will be frightened and probably angry with John. She may even rail at him, telling him it's his fault this has happened. She will not, however, go into a swoon and need smelling salts to get her back on her feet. If she was that type of woman she'd never have found the courage to leave John in the first place. She'll most likely join forces with John to help him find their child.

• Are points of view consistent? Are the scenes restricted to one viewpoint? If there is a point of view change within the scene, does it occur during a thought process or moment of decision that will cause the reader more worry? When the previous point of view is picked up, is it right where it left off? If not, have you provided for an appropriate time change? There are as many opinions on how points of view should be written as there are "how-to" books for writers. Some books will say you can't mix points of view in a scene, and other books will say you can. The best advice on points of view is to write them the way they come naturally for you. If you do mix points of view in a scene, look for even transitions to make sure it's clear to the reader whose point of view that portion of the scene is in.

- Do the scenes relate to the main story line (goals, motivations, and internal and external conflicts) that you wrote at the beginning of this critique? Make sure that your scenes reflect the storyline you set up in your first chapter. If John is seeking custody of his child, we don't want to suddenly be off exploring his interest in scuba diving. This doesn't mean John can't enjoy scuba diving, but if you're going to have a scuba diving scene, it should, in some way, relate to the story line.

EVALUATE ENDING

The ending of your book is as important as your beginning. In the opening of your story, you grab the reader's attention so that they want to keep reading and find out what happens to your characters. The ending needs to leave the reader satisfied and wanting more. If your beginning and your middle are fabulous but your ending is flat, you'll disappoint your reader. This could mean the difference between selling your manuscript and not selling it.

In order to make sure your ending isn't flat, ask yourself the following questions:

- Has the goal been accomplished? Remember, the goal probably won't be the goal you opened with in chapter one. You've most likely started out with your character seeking one goal but achieving another. But a definite goal, easily identified by the reader, must be achieved in order for the reader to be satisfied at the end of the book.

- Is the secret revealed, and how does it affect others at the end? In the beginning your character had a terrible secret that, if revealed, would cause her or a loved one irreparable harm. At the end, the secret should be revealed. Did it cause irreparable harm to your character or the people she loves, and if not, why not? Did your character or characters learn something when this secret was revealed? If so, what did they learn?

- Does the last "big black moment" demonstrate that the problem will be solved? The end of your story must have a "crisis" scene, where your protagonist is in battle to save, and possibly redeem, himself. This scene will look as if all is lost, but the character will somehow overcome the odds against him or her and win. This scene will probably be the prelude to the last scene in your book. In an earlier example, we discussed John running into a burning building to save his child. In the "big black moment" scene, John may get into the building and freeze. Then he overcomes his fear of fire and saves the child. During this scene, he may promise himself that if he gets out of this alive, he'll do the right thing. You want your reader cheering for your character to survive the "big black moment," so he can redeem himself.

EVALUATE SCENE STRUCTURE

Each scene, like the overall story, must have its own personal goal, which will carry the story forward yet bring its own conflict to the characters. These scenes keep the reader turning the pages, wanting to know what happens next. To make sure that your scenes move your story forward, ask yourself:

- Is the short-term goal of the scene stated at the beginning, either directly or indirectly? Not all scenes will state a direct goal, but they should indirectly support a goal already stated. For instance, the reader learns at the beginning of the story that John wants to get custody of his son by getting his ex-wife declared an unfit mother. In another scene, he starts asking the child subtle questions about his mother's care. The reader knows that John is trying to get ammunition from the child that he can use against the mother.

- Does the scene end with a setback for the main character(s) that forces him/them to change the previous short-term goal to a new one? In order to keep the reader's attention, you need a constant conflict for your character. Each scene either needs to be a form of conflict that is a setback and forces the protagonist to come up with a new goal, or it needs to be a scene which will set up your character to face a setback. For instance, let's say John has just learned that, while they were married, his ex-wife had an affair with his ex-business partner, and they experimented with drugs. He's ready to rush off to his attorney with the information, but his ex-business partner tells him that if John reveals the affair and the drug use, he'll tell the Securities and Exchange Commission about John using insider information to benefit in a big stock deal. This would destroy John's reputation in the business community, endanger his livelihood, and possibly land him in jail. He must, therefore, find another way to prove his wife an unfit mother.

- Do the transitions from scene to scene flow smoothly? Make sure each scene opens and closes in a way that feels natural to the reader. If you jolt your reader with an awkward transition, she will be pulled out of the story and may not get back into it. For instance, at the end of your scene, you have John confronting his business partner, but in your next scene you've jumped to two days later, and John's talking to his daughter's teacher. Your reader is going say, "Hey, wait a minute! What happened with the business partner?" Your reader is expecting to move through the story in a natural progression. If you skip a step, you'll chance losing your reader.

- Do your scenes end with a cliff hanger that makes the reader want to keep reading? You can't have every chapter end with a character in jeopardy, but each scene should end at a point where the reader says, "My word, what is he/she going to do now?" Many readers will read until the end of a scene, telling themselves that when they finish that scene they'll put down the book and go do something else. You want your scenes to be so compelling that the reader keeps saying, "Just one more page, and then I'll go start dinner or run errands or get on the treadmill." If you don't feel your scenes are fulfilling this goal, pull out a book you've read that you couldn't put down. Look at the scene endings and see how the writer was able to keep you turning the pages, even though you had something else you needed to do.

- Have you avoided coincidence? It's a bad idea to rely on coincidence in a story. Even in "real life" coincidence is rare. Most readers like to feel as if their characters are in charge of their lives, even if conflict keeps them from achieving their goals, because then the reader feels as if she also has control of her life. When you insert coincidence into a story, you make the reader feel as if the character is being controlled by some external force, which makes the reader uncomfortable. There can be a place for coincidence in a story, such as being in the wrong place at the wrong time. This is an excellent opening for a suspense or mystery book, where someone becomes involved in an event simply because he happened to be at the corner of River and Main when James Smith got shot. But in most instances, avoid coincidence.

- Are your characters spending a lot of time involved in a misunderstanding that could easily be resolved by simply talking? You've probably read books where two people end up in an argument, and the argument is dragged out through several chapters. You're ready to throw the book against the wall because if the characters would talk to each other for two minutes the argument would be resolved. Some writers will use this type of plot device, stating that it sustains conflict. This is not conflict. It's a contrived effort to fill space, and your readers will recognize it as such. Misunderstandings should be resolved quickly.

EVALUATE GRAMMAR AND SENTENCE STRUCTURE

If you don't feel you have good grammar skills, buy some grammar books to study, or take a continuing education course in grammar. Your grammar doesn't have to be perfect to get published, but it does have to be reasonably accurate. Good grammar and a clean, well typed or printed manuscript is as important a selling tool as your plot. If you feel your grammar is reasonably good and you have a computer, get a word processing program with a built-in grammar checker. Be aware, however, that most grammar checkers are geared toward business writing, and a spell-checker does not catch incorrect word usage. If you can't afford such a program, you don't have a computer, or you'd just rather do grammar checking yourself, ask yourself:

- Do you use active voice and strong verbs? Do you use action verbs for movement?

  Active voice: John ran to the corner, tripping on the curb as he tried to make the crossing light.

  Inactive voice: John was tripped by the curb as he tried to get across the street before the light changed.

- Do you show rather than tell?

  Show: John slammed his fist against his desk and said, . . .

  Tell: John was angry as he said, . . .

- Are the sentences varied? Look at your sentence structure. Make sure you don't start several sentences in a row with the same word. Try to mix short and long sentences, so you don't have too many of one or the other in one paragraph. Check for rhythm and tone by randomly picking out an occasional paragraph and reading it aloud. If you read several paragraphs and they don't sound right, you should carefully review your entire manuscript.

- Can you distinguish the characters through dialogue without the tags? Do you use a lot of "-ly" words or adverbs? Your characters should be so well developed that the reader can read a page of dialogue and know which character is speaking without a tag line. If you want to break up dialogue with a tag, stick to he said/she said. These tags do not draw attention to themselves, and the reader will not consciously notice them. Also, avoid using a lot of "-ly" words, such as, he laughed heartily; she said haughtily. Instead, say, he laughed, or he gave a hearty laugh. Her voice had a haughty tone when she said. . .

FINAL REVIEW

After you've finished your self-critique, put your manuscript away for another week or two. When you've gone through this second cooling off period, read the manuscript again. At this point, you should be able to decide whether it's ready to be mailed to an agent or an editor, or if it needs more work.

Do not, however, obsess over each word, action, and other detail in your manuscript. Constant revision will edit the life out of your story, and it will lose the magic it had when you first wrote it.

Another reason writers often keep revising is fear. They're looking for problems that will give them an excuse not to send the manuscript to an editor or an agent. If you find yourself sitting down to rewrite your manuscript again and again, ask yourself if you really feel the manuscript needs work, or if you are afraid that sending it out will result in rejection. If it's the latter reason, mail it out as fast as you can. Yes, you may get rejected, but a manuscript can't sell if it's sitting in your desk drawer or in a file on your computer.

APPENDIX A

CHECKLIST FOR CHOOSING (OR FORMING) A CRITIQUE GROUP

When you are thinking about joining a critique group, visit the group a few times and then consider this list of questions. If you are trying to form a critique group, give a list of these questions to potential members and use them to help establish guidelines for the group. Personalize the list by adding questions that meet your specific needs.

❑ Does the critique group require its members to produce a certain amount of work in order to belong to the group?

❑ How many members are in the group?

❑ Will I have enough time to review all of their work based upon the minimum page requirement?

❑ What type of writers are in the critique group?

❑ Does the group also brainstorm if members are

having problems with their current project or are starting a new project?

❑   Do I like the dynamics of the group?

❑   Other thoughts/questions:

_____

_____

_____

_____

_____

_____

_____

_____

_____

_____

_____

_____

_____

_____

_____

_____

_____

_____

APPENDIX B

BLUEPRINT CHECKLIST
FOR A CRITIQUE

Whether you're critiquing your own manuscript or someone else's, use this checklist to determine if the manuscript is on track.

❑   If this is a self-critique and you've finished your manuscript, have you put it away for one or more weeks? If not, do so now and *do not* continue with this list until at least one week has passed.

After your cooling off period, you can begin your critique by completing the following:

❑   **CHARACTER ANALYSIS**

❑   Can you identify the goals, motivations, and internal and external conflicts of your characters?

❑   Do the threads of your characters' goals,

motivations, and internal and external conflicts run through the manuscript?

❑   If your characters' goals, motivations and conflicts change in the story, are the reasons for change clearly defined?

❑   Establish a character chart of the book, such as the example below, to track where your characters appear in the manuscript and who interacts with them.

	BEGINNING			MIDDLE			END		
CHARACTER	ONE	TWO	THREE	FOUR	FIVE	SIX	SEVEN	EIGHT	NINE
Susan (Protagonist)	x	x	x	x	x	x	x	x	x
John (Antogonist)	x		x	x		x	x	x	x
Tom	x		x		x		x		x
Jane		x	x		x	x	x		x
Harry			x	x		x			

❑   Do you need to beef up a character?
❑   Downsize a minor character?
❑   Is a minor character, in reality, a major character, and you need to make changes to reflect that change?

❑   **BEGINNING:**

❑   Where does the story begin?

❑   Is it in the middle of action?

❑   Is what the protagonist believes to be true about himself being challenged or threatened?

❑   Does something happen to your protagonist in the first chapter that starts the clock ticking?

❑   What is the dramatic event in the beginning of the book that will threaten the main character and cause a change in his or her self-image?

❑   What is your main character's terrible secret that, if revealed, will cause him or someone he loves irreparable harm?

❑   What is his goal—the problem to be solved at the end of the book?

❑   How does your character intend to solve the problem in the beginning of the book?

❑   Are you happy with your opening scene? If not, look for the first action scene that hooks your interest. Should this be the opening scene?

❑   Can the information you're providing before the action scene be given in small flashbacks throughout the book?

❑   Did you set your clock so it will tick to an inevitable end?

❏   **MIDDLE:**

- ❏   Is the conflict increasing?
- ❏   Is your protagonist constantly facing obstacles that appear insurmountable?
- ❏   Are the characters changing?
- ❏   Why?
- ❏   Are the changes visible?
- ❏   Are the character's old motivations and goals replaced by new ones?
- ❏   Are the characters overreacting?
- ❏   Are their scenes dramatic and not melodramatic?
- ❏   Are points of view consistent?
- ❏   Are the scenes restricted to one viewpoint?
- ❏   If there is a point of view change within the scene, does it occur during a thought process or moment of decision that will cause the reader more worry?
- ❏   When the previous point of view is picked up, is it right where it left off?
- ❏   If not, have you provided for an appropriate time change?
- ❏   Do the scenes relate to the main story line (goals, motivations, and internal and external conflicts) that you wrote at the beginning of this critique?

❏   **ENDING:**

❏   Has the goal been accomplished?

❏   Is the secret revealed, and how does it affect others at the end?

❏   Did it cause irreparable harm to your character or the people they love?

❏   If not, why not?

❏   Did your character or characters learn something when this secret was revealed?

❏   If so, what did they learn?

❏   Does the last "big black moment" demonstrate that the problem will be solved?

❏   **SCENE STRUCTURE:**

❏   Is the short-term goal of the scene stated at the beginning, either directly or indirectly?

❏   Does the scene end with a setback for the main character(s) that forces him/them to change the previous short-term goal to a new one?

❏   Do the transitions from scene to scene flow smoothly?

❏   Does each scene open and close in a way that feels natural to the reader? Do your scenes end with a cliff hanger that makes the reader want to keep reading?

❏   Have you avoided coincidence?

❑   Are your characters spending a lot of time involved in a misunderstanding that could easily be resolved by simply talking?

❑   GRAMMAR AND SENTENCE STRUCTURE:

❑   Do you use active voice and strong verbs?
❑   Do you use action verbs for movement?
❑   Do you show rather than tell?
❑   Are the sentences varied?
❑   Can you distinguish the characters through dialogue without the tags?
❑   Do you use a lot of "-ly" words or adverbs?

❑   FINAL REVIEW:

After you've finished your critique, put your manuscript away for another week or two. When you've gone through this second cooling off period, read the manuscript again. At this point you should be able to decide whether it's ready to be mailed to an agent or an editor, or if it needs more work.

❏   **SPECIAL NOTES:**

_____

_____

_____

_____

_____

_____

_____

_____

_____

_____

_____

_____

_____

_____

_____

_____

_____

_____

_____

_____

_____

_____

_____

_____

_____

_____

APPENDIX C

The following scene is an example of line editing. A critique example of the same scene is on page 83.

EXAMPLE OF LINE EDITING

"Where is she?" John Exton cried out as Antonia Upton, his ex-wife opened the door to her office.

She stood there holding the door open staring up at the man she'd been practicing to hate for this past year. "Where is who?"

"Becky, our daughter Who did you think I was talking about?" He gazed at her fiercely as if she knew a secret and purposely kept him out. She was always like that. Open with people who didn't give a damn. Lousy with those who did.

Antonia stiffened, her back rigid at the edge of the door, but her voice was low and calm as she saw pairs of eyes gazing at them. As usual, John loved to instigate a scene. "Becky is in school. You are not supposed to have her till this weekend and . . ."

"Wrongo!" He said waving a piece of paper in front of her.

Antonia swallowed hard. A chill swept her up as quickly as if she'd been blasted with a sudden drop in temperature. "Let's go inside my office." She stood back to let him pass.

He stomped in but barely waited 'till she closed the door when he swung around at her, pushing the paper in front of her face.

She had an urge to slap him and wondered how he had ever made detective with his attitude. But now was not the time, she told herself. He was up to something, and she steeled herself to resist the yearning inside to touch him. She would not let him know she still cared, not after what he had put her through this past year. She took the paper from his hand and glanced at it. And her blood ran cold.

"What do you mean you have custody of Becky?" she said in a low, harsh tone as she dropped the paper to the floor. She glared at him. "What do you mean, where is she?"

"I've got custody. Becky is not in school."

Antonia turned toward her desk and started punching in the phone number. As she did, her finger slipped, and she had to repunch it again. She took several breaths as she waited for the someone to pick up the other end.

"This is Doctor Upton," she said.

"Oh, Doctor Upton," the school secretary blurted out. "I was just about to call you. You've got to come here as soon as possible. Please, hurry. We've got detectives here."

"Why? What happened?"

"It's Becky... she's gone!"

She didn't even realize the phone had dropped from her hand until she heard the loud crack coming from her desk. She turned to John.

"This wouldn't have happened if you hadn't taken a full-time position," John said accusingly. "I told you Becky was too fragile for you to leave her full time."

"What about you? Gone day and night?" she shouted at him. "Gone day and night! What kind of father does that to his only child?"

"A father who's trying to keep this world from harming her!"

"Go to hell," she spurted out. "I don't have time for this!" She grabbed her purse and coat and had started to run out the door when John stopped her.

"So you didn't hide her?" He said accusingly.

"Are you nuts? Why would I do that? Now get away from me!"She pushed him as she started to open the door.

But he held the door tight. "Becky ran away?"

Antonia froze at the thought. "She wouldn't. She's a diabetic. She needs her insulin. And she was... That's just not like her. She's been upset, but to run away?" She shook her head violently. "No, I don't believe it."

"You talking as a shrink or a mother?"

Antonia glared at him. "How dare you? Now get away from me before I..."

"Call the police? I am police."

"You're undercover, remember? Your drug scenes are more important. Your deals are more important. The rest of the world is more important than your family."

"And you didn't give a shit about Becky,

because if you did, you wouldn't have gone to work full time."

"And you're a jerk. Now get away from me or I'll blow your cover. And I can do it. I know you! I know who you are."

"And get me killed?"

"If that's what it takes to get you off mine and Becky's back. Now I want to go find out what's happened to our daughter. And you can't come with me unless you want to blow your cover."

He glared at her, saw the moistness in her eyes and finally stepped back. She was right. He was so close to getting the two bastards locked up that he couldn't risk anything now. And she was just mean enough to do it. How the hell did he had ever manage d to fall in love with her was a mystery. And she still had that pull. He hated it, hated himself for wanting to kiss her now, violently, angrily, to show her that she couldn't control him. And yet, that's exactly what would tell her she did control him. Gritting his teeth and fighting back the need to grab her to him, he forecefully stepped back.

Antonia swung the door, almost hitting him in his face, as she stomped out of her office. At the same time, his beeper went off. He glanced at the phone number. Damn. It was one of his agents using a number that was an emergency. He snapped the door shut, went for the phone and punched in the number.

"What?" He said.

"Pardon me, Sir," Jack's voice came over the phone as if far away. "But you're in big trouble."

"They know?"

"Yep, and they're coming after you as I'm speaking. They got your kid and they're after you next."

John heard a scream outside Antonia's door and a shot of gunfire. He threw the phone down and ran for the window, lifting it. Outside, the second story window had was no fire escape, just enough of a ledge to get him past the office. And he wasn't sure he'd even make it. In the distance, across the street, he saw Antonia's car turn left and a huge relief ran through over him. They had missed her. Then he saw the truck parked below. A truck filled with mattresses. He jumped and heard shots wing past him. As he hit the mattresses, he rolled over swiftly, jumping down off the truck when a shot grazed his upper arm. Blood started oozing out. "Damn," he said as he fell onto the ground. He looked up. There, standing in the window was JawMan, pointing an AK 45 right into his face.

EXAMPLE OF A CRITIQUE

This is a great scene. You grabbed my attention right from the beginning, and I particularly liked the sentence in paragraph two, where you said: *the man she'd been practicing to hate for this past year.* I also liked paragraph three, where you said: *She was always like that. Open with people who didn't give a damn. Lousy with those who did.* This told me volumes about these two characters and why they are antagonistic towards each other.

Some of the problems I saw were:

1. You wrote: *He gazed at her fiercely as if she knew a secret and purposely kept him out. She was always like that. Open with people who didn't give a damn. Lousy with those who did.*

Comment: As I said above, I love the last three lines of this section. The first line, however, appears to be in Antonia's POV, while the last three lines appear to be in John's POV. You may want to rewrite the first line so that it's in John's point of view.

2. You wrote: *"Wrongo!" He said waving a piece of paper in front of her.*

Comment: The word "Wrongo" did not seem like the type of word a macho, undercover police officer would use.

3. You wrote: *"What do you mean you have custody of Becky?" she said in a low, harsh tone as she dropped the paper to the floor. She glared at him. "What do you mean, where is she?"*

"I've got custody. Becky is not in school."

Comment: This section was confusing. Antonia has just learned that John was granted custody of Becky. Why would Antonia ask him where Becky is? At the beginning of the scene, John accused her of hiding Becky, but Antonia thinks Becky's in school. Since she doesn't know Becky's missing until she calls the school, it would seem the shock of her finding out John has custody would override his accusation that she's hiding Becky.

You may want to lengthen this part of the scene slightly so that Antonia can be hit with the shock of his getting custody. Then he could again accuse her of hiding Becky. She could tell him that's ridiculous, that she didn't even know he filed for custody, so why would she hide her? Then she could call the school.

4. You wrote: *"Oh, Doctor Upton," the school secretary blurted out. "I was just about to call you. You've got to come here as soon as possible. Please, hurry. We've got detectives here. "*

"Why? What happened?"

"It's Becky.... she's gone!"

Comment: It seems odd that the school secretary would say there were detectives at the school without first saying that

Becky is missing. You may want to have the secretary state that Becky's missing and then reveal that the police detectives are there.

5. You wrote: *She didn't even realize the phone dropped from her hand until she heard the loud crack coming from her desk.*

Comment: It took me a moment to realize that the loud crack was caused by the phone hitting the desk. You may want to change it to something like: the loud crack it made as it hit her desk.

6. Look at the scene from the paragraph starting with: *"This wouldn't have happened if you hadn't taken a full-time position,"* to the paragraph starting with: *Antonia froze at the thought.*

Comment: It seemed odd that Antonia didn't realize the moment she talked to the school that Becky ran away. John has stormed in accusing her of hiding the child, and the school's just said that she's missing. Wouldn't she immediately leap to the conclusion that Becky ran away? Also, wouldn't John, seeing Antonia's reaction to learning from the school that Becky's missing, realize that he was wrong about Antonia? Wouldn't he think that Becky must have run away? Also, he later learns that Becky's been kidnapped. Would he consider this possibility when he realizes Antonia isn't involved?

7. You wrote: *John heard a scream outside Antonia's door and a shot of gunfire. He threw the phone down and ran for the window, lifting it. Outside, the second story window had was no fire escape, just enough of a ledge to get him past the office. And he wasn't sure he'd even make it. In the distance, across the street, he saw Antonia's car turn left and a huge relief ran over him. They had missed her.*

Comment: Where did the scream or shot come from? In

the building (outside Antonia's office door) or from the street? If it's in the building, wouldn't John rush to the reception area to see what's happened? He is a police officer. Also, he was just told that someone kidnaped his daughter and is after him. Wouldn't he think they might also try to grab Antonia? If you want him trapped so he must use the window to escape, you should consider having him at least open the office door and look into the reception area before running to the window.

If the shots come from the street, when he runs to the window, wouldn't he look down to see where the shot's are coming from before thinking about a fire escape and ledge? And if they did come from outside, why can't he use the door instead of jumping? You may want to have bad guys both in the office and outside the building.

If John's trapped in Antonia's office, once he sees Antonia's car leaving, he can realize she's safe and then worry about the ledge. Also, how can he be sure Antonia's driving the car? Should you let him get a glimpse of her behind the wheel so he knows it's her and she's safe?

6. In the last paragraph of this scene you have JawMan pointing an AK 45 into John's face. Are you sure there's such a weapon as an AK 45? I've always heard the words AK 47, but I'm not a weapons expert. If you haven't already, you may want to check this out.

Those were the problems I saw in the scene. If you have any questions, I'll be happy to answer them.

AFTERWORD

Hopefully, this book has given you the guidelines you need to determine if:

- You can handle a critique of your work.
- You can give an effective critique of someone else's work.
- What type of critique group you need, or if you should have a critique partner or perform self-critiques.

All of the above items are critical, but the most important question you need to ask yourself is: *Will a critique of my work make me a better writer?*

Consider the question carefully and answer it honestly. If criticism depresses you to the point that you find it difficult to work, then you should stay away from any form of critique. I've known writers who have joined critique groups or become a critique partner because they felt pressured by other writers to do so. They felt that if everyone else could "take it" so could they, even though they knew deep down that they couldn't. Sadly, many of these writers stopped writing because the criticism was more than they could handle and destroyed what little self-confidence they had in their writing. If they'd just said "no" they might be on the New York Times Bestsellers list today. Now they'll never know if they could have made it.

The most important job of a writer is to keep focused on making your writing dreams come true, whether it's the dream of completing a manuscript for the first time, getting published, or making it to the New York Times Bestseller's list. A critique group or partnership is simply a tool that may help you achieve those dreams.

ABOUT THE AUTHOR

National best selling and award winning author, Linda Griffin, who writes under the pen names Carin Rafferty and Allyson Ryan, has sixteen published novels to her credit. *The Writer's Guide to Critique Groups* is the first book released by her own publishing imprint, ImaJinn Books.

Linda is currently at work on a book for Gryphon Books For Writers, which is tentatively titled, *Pitching Your Manuscript to Editors and Agents*, and should be available in the Summer of 2000.

ATTENTION
ROMANCE AUTHORS

ImaJinn (pronounced Imagine) Books publishes supernatural, paranormal, fantasy, futuristic, and time travel romances. We are looking for fast-paced, action-packed stories involving ghosts, psychics and/or psychic phenomena, witches, vampires, werewolves, angels, reincarnation, futuristic in space or on other planet, futuristic on earth, time travel to the past, and time travel to the present. All novels should be atmospheric in accord with the chosen subject. Most stories should be dark and frightening, although lighter story lines will be considered, particularly in stories involving angels, futuristics and time travel.

The developing romantic relationship between the hero and the heroine is the focus of the story. The stories may be told from both points of view, and the hero may be the lead character of the story. Although books written in the third person are preferred, first person will be considered. Sensuality may range from sweet to highly sensual.

The heroine must be a strong woman, capable of confronting and conquering any threats of physical and/or psychological danger she faces in the story. She is always a match for the hero who should be bold and brash (a definite alpha-type), and he may or may not represent danger. Their relationship, and the danger to that relationship, should keep the reader on the edge of her/his seat and send shivers up her/his spine. The ending must be a happy one with everlasting romance the reward for triumphing over the darkness or evil faced in the story.

LENGTH: 60,000 to 100,000 words

SUBMISSION: You do not need an agent to submit your story. It is recommended that you either e-mail or call ImaJinn Books to see what types of books they're currently looking for. If you have a book that meets their current needs, query first. All query letters should include a synopsis no longer than five double-spaced pages. Query letters may be submitted by regular mail or e-mail. If submitted by regular mail, include an SASE.

Query letters or inquiries should be sent to:

ImaJinn Books
PO Box 162
Hickory Corners, MI 49060-0162
Phone: (616) 671-4633
E-mail: imajinn@worldnet.att.net

Blue Diamond Publications
2429 Obetz Drive
Beavercreek OH 45434-6931
1-800-721-8311   (937) 320-1642 (fax)
e-mail: bluediamond@usa.net

Name: _____
Address: _____
City, State, Zip Code: _____
Telephone (Voice/Fax): _____
E-Mail: _____

QTY	DESCRIPTION	TOTAL
	Enchanted Journeys Beyond the Imagination, Vol 1, Spiral bound, May-95, ISBN 0-9647291-0-5, Stock # RBV1, **$24.95**	
	Enchanted Journeys Beyond the Imagination, Vol 2, Spiral bound, May-96, ISBN 0-9647291-1-3, Stock # RBV2, **$24.95**	
	Enchanted Journeys Beyond the Imagination, Vol 3, Spiral bound, Aug-97, ISBN 0-9647291-4-8, Stock # RBV3, **$24.95**	
	Enchanted Journeys Beyond the Imagination, Vol 4, Spiral	
	Enchanted Journeys Beyond the Imagination, Vols 1&2 Combined,	
	SAVE $9.95! Buy any 2 **Enchanted Journeys Beyond the Imagi-**	
	BUY 3 GET 1 FREE! Buy **Enchanted Journeys Beyond the Imagi-nation**	
	Enchanted Journeys Beyond the Imagination Master Index, Vols. 1-4, Apr-99, ISBN 0-9647291-6-4, Stock # MI02, **$9.95**	
	The Alternate Reality Romance Guide, Spiral bound, Apr-98, 175 pages, 8-1/2" x 11", ISBN 0-9647291-7-2, Stock # RBD1, **$54.95**	
	Scene of the Crime, Vol 1, Spiral bound, Mar-99, ISBN 0-9647291-8-0, Stock # MB01, **$24.95**	

Second Day Air		Book Rate		Order Sub-total	
1 Bk	$4.00	1 Bk	$2.25	Ohio Residents, add 6% Sales Tax	
2 Bks	$7.00	2 Bks	$3.75	Shipping	
3 Bks	NA	3 Bks	$5.00	ORDER TOTAL	

MONEY BACK GUARANTEE IF NOT COMPLETELY SATISFIED!

Return completed order form and check, MO or Credit Card (Discover, Master Card, Visa), payable to **Blue Diamond Publications**, to Dept. IP-01 the address above.